W9-AHG-817

What Is the Theory of Plate Tectonics?

Craig Saunders

Crabtree Publishing Company

www.crabtreebooks.com

SHAPING MODERN SCIENCE

Author: Craig Saunders
Publishing plan research and development:
   Sean Charlebois, Reagan Miller
   Crabtree Publishing Company
Editors: Renata Brunner Jass, Adrianna Morganelli
Proofreaders: Gina Springer Shirley, Molly Aloian
Project coordinator: Kathy Middleton
Editorial services: Clarity Content Services
Production coordinator and prepress technician:
   Katherine Berti
Print coordinator: Katherine Berti
Series consultant: Eric Walters
Cover design: Katherine Berti
Design: First Image
Photo research: Linda Tanaka

Illustrations: Joanna Rankin

Photographs: title page/cover bottom © The Natural History Museum/ Alamy; cover top right Shutterstock; cover top left Jeremy Bishop/Photo Researchers, Inc.; p5 NASA Goddard Space Flight Center; p6 NASA; p8 Eduard Lebiedzki, after a design by Carl Rahl/public domain/wiki; p9 Public domain/wiki; p10 Denise Kappa/Shutterstock; p11 top Amateria 1121 licensed under the Creative Commons Attribution-Share Alike 3.0 Unported license, Forest Service of the United States Dept of Agriculture; p12, 13 Public domain/wiki; p14 edella/Shutterstock; p15 Public domain/ wiki; p16 Rudi Gobbo/iStock; p17 CCL/wiki; p18 top Moondigger licensed under the Creative Commons Attribution-Share Alike 2.5 Generic license, Zephyris licensed under the Creative Commons Attribution-Share Alike 3.0 Unported license, SNP licensed under the Creative Commons Attribution-Share Alike 3.0 Unported license, p19 top Mila licensed under the Creative Commons Attribution-Share Alike 3.0 Unported, 2.5 Generic, 2.0 Generic and 1.0 Generic license, Michael S. Engel licensed under the Creative Commons Attribution 3.0 Unported license, Slade Winstone (Sladew) licensed under the Creative Commons Attribution-Share Alike 3.0 Unported, 2.5 Generic, 2.0 Generic and 1.0 Generic license; p20 USGS; p21 Moltenrock licensed under the Creative Commons Attribution-Share Alike 2.5 Generic, 2.0 Generic and 1.0 Generic license; p22 Lya_Cattel/iStock; p23 Yummifruitbat licensed under the Creative Commons Attribution-Share Alike 2.5 Generic license; p26 plavusa87/Shutterstock; p29 Public domain/wiki; p30 Craig Saunders; p31 Mbz1 at en.wikipedia licensed under the Creative Commons Attribution-Share Alike 3.0 Unported, 2.5 Generic, 2.0 Generic and 1.0 Generic license; p33 NOAA; p35 USGS; p36 USGS; p37 Vakhrushev Pavel/Shutterstock, Circumnavigation/Shutterstock; p38 Tatiana Grozetskaya/ Shutterstock; p39 left clockwise USGS, Siim Sepp 2006 licensed under the Creative Commons Attribution-Share Alike 3.0 Unported license, Photograph taken by Mark A. Wilson (Department of Geology, The College of Wooster) released by author into the public domain/wiki; p42 top Canadian Loon/ BigStock, granitepeaker/BigStock; p43 top hsean05/BigStock, granite-peaker/BigStock, 104paul/BigStock; p44 2007 David Monniaux licensed under the Creative Commons Attribution-Share Alike 3.0 Unported license; p45 left clockwise Mila Zinkova licensed under the Creative Commons Attribution-Share Alike 3.0 Unported, 2.5 Generic, 2.0 Generic and 1.0 Generic license, mikeuk/iStock, Barbara Page licensed under the Creative Commons Attribution-ShareAlike 3.0 License; p46 Chee-Onn Leong/Shutterstock; p50 USGov Dept of the Interior; p51 Andrei Nekrassov/Shutterstock; p52 NOAA; p53 NASA; p54-55 ginevre/iStock; p56 Vulkanette/Shutterstock.

Library and Archives Canada Cataloguing in Publication

Saunders, Craig, 1972-
    What is the theory of plate tectonics? / Craig Saunders.

(Shaping modern science)
Includes index.
Issued also in electronic format.
ISBN 978-0-7787-7202-6 (bound).--ISBN 978-0-7787-7209-5 (pbk.)

    1. Plate tectonics--Juvenile literature. 2. Geology, Structural--Juvenile literature. I. Title. II. Series: Shaping modern science

QE511.4.S29 2011   j551.1'36   C2011-900172-1

Library of Congress Cataloging-in-Publication Data

Saunders, Craig, 1972-
    What is the theory of plate tectonics? / Craig Saunders.
        p. cm. -- (Shaping modern science)
    Includes index.
    ISBN 978-0-7787-7202-6 (reinforced lib. bdg. : alk. paper) --
    ISBN 978-0-7787-7209-5 (pbk. : alk. paper) --
    ISBN 978-1-4271-9531-9 (electronic (PDF))
    1. Plate tectonics--Juvenile literature. 2. Geology, Structural--Juvenile literature. I. Title. II. Series.

QE511.4.S288 2011
551.1'36--dc22
                                            2010052622

Crabtree Publishing Company

www.crabtreebooks.com   1-800-387-7650

Printed in the U.S.A./022011/CJ20101228

Published in Canada
Crabtree Publishing
616 Welland Ave.
St. Catharines, ON
L2M 5V6

Published in the United States
Crabtree Publishing
PMB 59051
350 Fifth Avenue, 59th Floor
New York, New York 10118

Published in the United Kingdom
Crabtree Publishing
Maritime House
Basin Road North, Hove
BN41 1WR

Published in Australia
Crabtree Publishing
386 Mt. Alexander Rd.
Ascot Vale (Melbourne)
VIC 3032

Contents

What Is the Theory of Plate Tectonics?

The ground beneath your feet is constantly moving. The Earth's surface is made up of solid sections of rock called plates, which float on a more liquid layer beneath them. You can't see them move, but sometimes you can feel earthquakes that result from the plates crashing into each other.

In studying the shapes of the **continents**, the makeup of rocks, and **fossil** records, scientists gradually developed the Theory of Plate Tectonics. More recently, scientists have been able to regularly monitor the movement of the plates.

The Theory of Plate Tectonics explains how the lighter, solid plates that form the Earth's crust (or surface) float on denser material just below the crust. The plates move apart, opening up oceans or valleys; crash into each other, thrusting up mountains; or push under one another, creating volcanoes.

The Earth and Its Structure

The Earth is not completely solid. Much of it is actually made up of molten (liquid) rock.

Earth has four layers. In the solid inner core, rock is very dense and contains large amounts of the metals nickel and iron. The liquid outer core is about 1,400 miles (2,260 km) thick. Further out is the mantle, a layer of hot, mostly solid material about 1,770 miles (2,850 km) thick. The solid crust is very thin compared to the other layers. It is at most 25 miles (40 km) thick, and usually much thinner. If your body were the Earth, the crust would be your skin.

Quick fact

Canada is home to the oldest known rocks in the world. A patch of rock on Hudson Bay formed 4.28 billion years ago

Rocks are made up of many **elements**, primarily iron, oxygen, silicon, and magnesium. When rocks melt, the elements separate. Heavy ones, particularly iron, tend to sink, which is why the core is so dense. Lighter ones, such as silicon and aluminum, tend to float, which is why they are abundant in the crust.

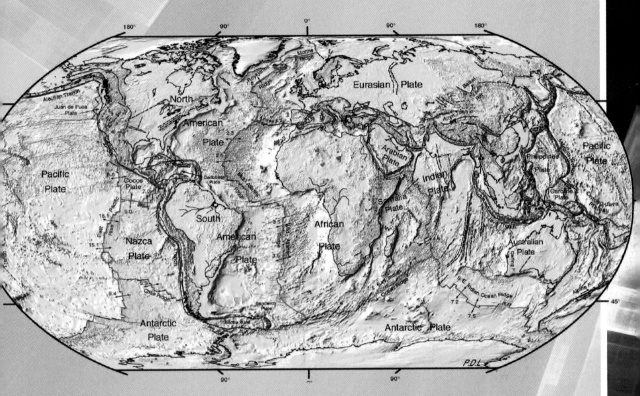

↑ This map of Earth shows earthquake and volcanic activity for the past one million years.

Scientific Theory or Law?

In science, a *theory* is a well-tested set of ideas that explains how something occurs. For example, many kinds of evidence together support the Theory of Plate Tectonics. A scientific *law* describes how something consistently happens under certain conditions. For example, the law of gravity describes how objects fall to Earth's surface.

Is Earth Unique?

Our **solar system** began as a vast cloud of gas and dust. About 4.56 billion years ago, gravity caused the dust and gas to form clumps. Most of the material gathered in the center. This clump became denser and hotter, and a **nuclear reaction** began. The result was the huge, radiating Sun we know today.

Material left over from the Sun's formation became the planets. The inner planets—Mercury, Venus, Earth, and Mars—were very hot. Many lighter elements boiled and were swept away by solar winds, leaving these planets dense and iron-rich. The gravity of the larger outer planets—Jupiter, Saturn, Uranus, and Neptune—captured much of the lighter material.

Extinct volcanoes, mountains, and other signs of a **dynamic** crust have been identified on Mercury, Venus, and Mars. Our Moon also looks like it had plates that moved, before it cooled and most activity stopped about three billion years ago. Earth appears to be the only planet that is still tectonically active.

↑ Our solar system includes the Sun, eight planets, several dwarf planets, asteroids, comets, rocks, and dust.

Shifting Plates and Life

The processes at work in plate tectonics probably also helped create Earth's atmosphere. The air we breathe and the hydrogen and oxygen that make water may once have been contained in rocks. As heat from the early Earth's core melted those rocks, it would have released those elements and forced them to the surface.

Today, the same heat still drives molten rock toward the surface. The heat causes the mantle and crust to move. So, heat movement not only makes mountains and ocean basins, but it also carries important **minerals** to the surface. Deep in the ocean, where sunlight cannot reach, scientists have found abundant life where hot, mineral-rich gases push through the crust.

How Old Is the Theory of Plate Tectonics?

While the process of plate tectonics is as old as the Earth itself, the theory only became established in the 1960s. Before that, people thought the continents were fixed in place.

In this book, we explore early theories about the Earth's surface and investigate how those ideas changed as scientists learned more about our planet.

"All earth sciences must contribute evidence towards unveiling the state of our planet in earlier times, and. . .the truth of the matter can only be reached by combining all this evidence."

—Alfred Wegener, interdisciplinary German scientist, in *The Origins of Continents and Oceans*, 1915

Quick fact

Our **universe** formed about 12–14 billion years ago. Our own solar system is thought to be much younger, about 4.5 billion years old.

A Flat Earth?

People have always tried to explain how oceans and mountains form. As people have learned more about the Earth, our ideas have changed.

Strange as it may seem, people's understanding of how the Earth works began with the idea that the planet is flat and floats on a pillow of air. About 2,500 years ago in Greece, the philosopher Anaxagoras tried to explain the universe. He thought the universe began as one big **mass** made of all the same material.

According to Anaxagoras, a powerful mind started everything rotating. That spinning made the material break up and then re-form, creating planets and stars. Heavier material pushed to the center and lighter material, such as fire, was thrown to the edges, he said. Earth was at the center of it all. That explained why the Earth was made of heavy materials, such as iron. He thought the Sun was a lump of fiery metal and the Moon was made of reflective earth.

Anaxagoras said the Earth was so heavy that it stayed where it was and did not spin. He also thought Earth floated on air. Because Earth is flat, he believed, water could spread evenly over its surface, with rivers being caused by evaporation and rain. Sometimes the air holding Earth up would get into cracks in the ground. When it became trapped, the moving air forced its way out, causing earthquakes.

↓ Anaxagoras was a Greek philosopher in the fifth century B.C.

Looking back today, it is easy to see the mistakes Anaxagoras made. However, he also got several things right, or at least partly right. Rotation is part of planet and star formation, just not quite the way he saw it. Solar systems and galaxies **rotate**, but around stars rather than the Earth. Natural objects are made up of particles, though not the ones he identified. He was also the first person to correctly explain **eclipses**. The Earth, though, is not flat. He got that part wrong, and he wasn't alone in doing so.

→Mappa mundi, *Map of the World from the mid-1400s: people of many ancient cultures believed the Earth was flat.*

The Seas Pour Into Darkness

To a person standing on the Earth's surface, the Earth may indeed look flat. For thousands of years, people accepted what they saw as truth. There were some minor differences from place to place. In ancient China, Earth was believed to be a flat square under round heavens. Ancient Greeks thought the earth was flat, circular, and floating on air.

Even the Vikings thought the world was flat, and they were great explorers. They were the first Europeans to travel to North America. Their legends say that this world, which they called Midgard, was a disk. In the middle was an area made out of the eyebrows of a giant named Ymir. Sail to the edge and you would fall off, where the seas poured off the world and into darkness. But before getting there, you would probably be swallowed by the giant sea serpent that circled the world.

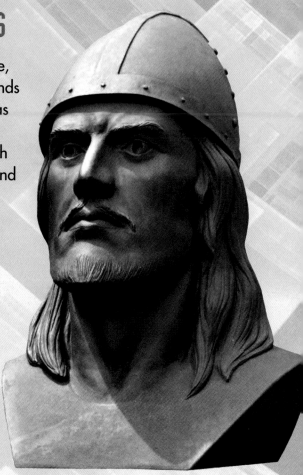

↑Although the Vikings explored large areas of the northern hemisphere by boat, they believed the world was flat.

"[The world] is ring-shaped without, and round about her without lieth the deep sea; and along the strand of that sea they gave lands to the races of giants for habitation. But on the inner earth they made a citadel round about the world against the hostility of the giants, and for their citadel they raised up the brows of Ymir the giant, and called that place Midgard."

—from *The Prose Edda*, by Snorri Sturluson

Native North Americans

Like the ancient Norse and Greeks, many Native American tribes have traditional stories that describe the planet and its formation. In North America, one of the most common legends tells of a huge flood. A new world was made from earth raised from the bottom of the sea. The ball of earth was put onto the back of a turtle and it grew into our world, held up by the turtle.

↑Native American legend tells that when Napi, the Creator, was finished creating the world, he crawled to the top of Turtle Mountain in Alberta and disappeared.

In many cases, evidence of plate tectonics can be found in stories about the world's beginning. Because of active fault lines, California experiences many earthquakes. In one Maidu legend from northern California, Coyote says he will tug on a rope from time to time to make the earth move. Some scientists study these legends to find clues about earthquakes, volcanoes, and tsunamis that happened before there were ways to measure and record them.

↑In the traditional cultures of several Native American tribes, the Black Hills of South Dakota and Wyoming are considered the sacred center of the world. The hills formed during the same mountain-building event that created the Rockies.

A Round Earth

In ancient times, many societies thought the Earth was flat. But the idea that Earth is a sphere is far from new. The great philosopher Aristotle was one of the first people to write about a spherical Earth. He lived in Greece between 384 B.C. and 322 B.C.

Like Anaxagoras, Aristotle thought Earth was the center of the universe and everything **revolved** around it. But he also realized that stars he saw in the north were different from the ones he saw in the south. That helped him understand that Earth is a sphere.

Aristotle also found fish fossils in the mountains. They helped him understand that land can be raised and then get washed away by wind, rain, and rivers. Today, we call those processes **uplifting** and **erosion**.

After Aristotle, the idea of a round Earth became widespread. Eratosthenes, who lived around 200 B.C., figured out the size of the Earth. He measured the distance between two cities and their angles relative to the Sun. He calculated that the planet is about 22,798 miles (39,690 km) around. Amazingly, our measurements today are almost the same.

→ *This image shows a nineteenth-century reconstruction of Eratosthenes' map of the known world around 194 B.C.*

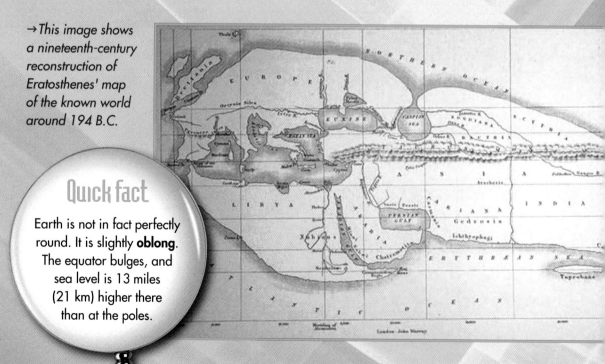

Quick fact

Earth is not in fact perfectly round. It is slightly **oblong**. The equator bulges, and sea level is 13 miles (21 km) higher there than at the poles.

The first big book of geography was written about 300 years after Aristotle died. It was written by Strabo, who grew up in what is now Turkey. His book, *Geography*, describes the **landforms** he saw during his travels through Egypt, Rome, parts of Asia, and many other places.

Strabo watched a volcano erupt. His theory was that hot winds beneath the ground blasted up, causing the volcano. They carried fire, ash, dust, and steam with them. We know today that volcanoes are caused by hot magma pushing up through the crust.

↑ *Strabo wrote detailed descriptions of the lands he visited. He died in the first century A.D.*

Quick fact

Earth's radius is 3,959 miles (6,374 km). Circumference equals the radius times two, multiplied by pi (3.14). That is 3,959 x 2 x π, so Earth is about 24,862 miles (40,029 km) around.

The Sun: Size Matters

The pull of the Sun's gravity keeps Earth, the planets, and the whole solar system in **orbit**. The more mass an object has, the more force it exerts on surrounding objects. The Sun is the most massive object in the solar system. That is why it is the center of the solar system.

Mount Vesuvius

One morning in the year A.D. 79, people in Pompeii woke up as usual. For many in this town in southern Italy, it would be the last time they would do so. At about noon, the mountain above them exploded.

Mount Vesuvius is a volcano. Its famous eruption buried Pompeii under more than 9 feet (2.8 m) of volcanic ash.

A teenager known as Pliny the Younger witnessed the eruption. He was one of the few people to escape the hot ash, poisonous gases, and lava that spewed from the mountaintop.

He later wrote:

"It shot up to a great height in the form of a tall trunk, which spread out at the top as though into branches. . . . Occasionally it was brighter, occasionally darker and spotted, as it was either more or less filled with earth and cinders."

More than 200 years before the eruption, Strabo had visited Mount Vesuvius. From the cinder-like rocks, he figured out the mountain began as a volcano. Because it had not erupted for hundreds of years, though, people felt safe living below it.

↓*Mount Vesuvius is a composite volcano on the Bay of Naples, Italy. It is the only volcano on mainland Europe to have erupted in the past century.*

Copernicus

The Greeks added a lot to our understanding of the Earth. However, it was nearly 1,500 years after Aristotle before people understood that the Sun is the center of the solar system. Nicolaus Copernicus wrote about this idea just before he died in 1543.

Copernicus spent his life watching the stars and planets. He realized they moved in more complicated ways than people had thought; the planets could not be revolving around the Earth. He created a new model of the solar system with the Sun in the center. He showed that Earth and the other planets revolved around the Sun in circular orbits. Religious leaders said his theories were impossible because they made a Bible-based understanding of the universe impossible.

↑Astronomer and mathematician Nicolaus Copernicus (1473–1543) realized that the planets' motions meant they must revolve around the Sun. This map illustrates Copernicus's vision of a sun-centered solar system.

People continued to study the stars and planets, and proved that the sun-centric theory was true. Copernicus changed the way we see our solar system. His theories also changed the way we understand how our planet works.

In the Beginning

Years of the Flood?

About the same time as Copernicus discovered that Earth orbits around the Sun, Leonardo da Vinci (1452–1519) made important discoveries about Earth's fossil record. Da Vinci spent a lot of time studying fossils near his home in northern Italy. He noticed that the same fossils showed up in the same kind of rock over large areas.

In the fifteenth century, many people believed that the Earth was once covered in water. This was a popular view, and one that seemed to be backed up by the Bible's story of Noah's Ark. But that didn't satisfy da Vinci. He found fossil coral, a kind of sea creature, at the top of mountains. He knew water flowed downhill, so any evidence of a flood should be in lower layers of rock, not on mountaintops. Also, he wondered, where would all the flood water have gone? He thought the flood stories might be wrong. But da Vinci never published his research, so it was centuries before his ideas were known.

↑This 236-million-year-old ammonite fossil was found in the Italian Alps. It formed in rocks on the seafloor, which were eventually pushed up as continental drift caused mountains to rise.

Quick fact

The Leonardo da Vinci who studied fossils is the same da Vinci, the artist, famous for painting the Mona Lisa.

What Goes on Top Stays on Top

↑Horizontal **sedimentary rock** layers are visible in the Grand Canyon, Arizona. The layers at the bottom are the oldest, and the uppermost layers are the youngest.

In the 1600s, Nicholas Steno discovered many of the same things da Vinci had recorded 200 years earlier. Steno wondered how solid objects such as fossils or **crystals** could get inside rocks. The answer, he suggested, was that all rocks were once fluid. If they were fluid, they would flow and harden into flat layers. This idea is the basis of two of **geology**'s most important principles.

Principle of Original Horizontality

When layers of rock are laid down, they form horizontal layers, or beds.

Law of Superposition

When layers of rock are laid down, the oldest layer will be on the bottom and the youngest layer on top.

More Than Just Sediment

Rocks can break apart and into smaller pieces, called particles. This process is called **weathering**. Rock particles washed away by water are called **sediment**. When the water reaches a flat area, as in a lake or ocean, it slows down. The sediment settles to the bottom. Over time, the weight of more and more deposits can turn the sediment into new rock, called sedimentary rock.

Dead plants and animals are often deposited with sediments. These become the fossils we find in sedimentary rock.

↑Cells in a tree's wood were replaced with minerals over millions of years, forming this **petrified** tree log.

←Soft plant parts, such as this gingko leaf, are sometimes preserved in sedimentary rock.

↓Ammonites were a type of cephalopod, distantly related to squid. All ammonites are extinct and known only from the fossil record.

Quick fact

Amber is fossilized resin from a tree. Because it began as a sticky liquid, amber often preserves ancient insects and pollen.

8

What Is a Fossil?

Fossils are the remains of plants or animals that lived long ago. Most are at least 10,000 years old, but some are more than a billion years old. Most are of sea creatures, because life on land did not exist until roughly 350 million years ago. Shells and bones are the most common because they do not break down easily.

↑ This fossil shrimp is found in Cretaceous-age sedimentary rock.

The Fossil Record

Fossils are one of the best sources of information about the past. In 1793, a British surveyor named William Smith realized that he could figure out how old a rock was by looking at the fossils in it. Everywhere he went in England, he found the same fossils in the same rock layers. The oldest fossils were always on the bottom and the youngest on top.

↑ This Leptofoenus pittfieldae, an extinct species of wasp, was preserved in amber. Amber is fossilized tree sap.

Early geologists spent a lot of time studying sedimentary rocks. They did not yet know how old the rocks were. However, fossils allowed them to understand newly discovered rocks. The different fossils in each layer let them figure out which were older or younger rocks.

→ This Eocene fossil flower is from Florissant Fossil Quarry, Florissant, Colorado, USA.

Rocks from Magma

It was easy for early geologists to figure out how sedimentary rocks formed. But that idea did not explain all rocks.

Many early geologists believed Earth was once covered in water. Abraham Werner (1749–1817), who studied the minerals in rocks, was one of them. He said rocks made up of crystals were from the beginning of the planet's history. He believed the crystals that made up these rocks formed in ancient oceans. Newer sedimentary rocks covered the older, crystalline ones.

↓Magma pouring from undersea rifts cools quickly into structures called pillow basalt.

Basalt

Basalt is a dark-colored rock made up of tiny crystals. It is the most common **igneous rock** on Earth. Because there are no fossils in basalt, it was one of the rocks that helped geologists realize that some rocks are not sedimentary.

Basalt has small crystals because it cools quickly. On land it forms from lava pouring out of volcanoes. At the bottom of the ocean, it can ooze up from cracks. There it cools very quickly and is called pillow basalt because of its shape.

↑The flow pattern of the lava that formed this basalt is still visible.

In the 1700s, that idea began to change. Abbé Anton Moro (1687–1750) studied volcanic islands and came up with the idea that there were two kinds of rocks. He said there were sedimentary rocks and rocks from volcanoes. Later in the century, a geologist named James Hutton (1726–1797) supported this view. He said there were two processes at work. There were sedimentary rocks formed by erosion and **deposition**. Then sedimentary rock was sometimes forced up into new mountains by heat and pressure. There were also other rocks that came from volcanoes. Those rocks are made from rocks that melted inside the earth.

Today we know that there are two main kinds of rock formed from molten rock. These are called **igneous rocks**. Ones with tiny crystals, such as basalt, come out of volcanoes. They have small crystals because they cooled quickly. Ones with larger crystals, such as granite, cooled slowly inside the Earth's crust.

Rocks That Change

James Hutton is often called the founder of modern geology. He published a book in 1795 called *Theory of the Earth with Proof and Illustrations*. This book contains many of the theories geologists rely on today.

Hutton's most important contribution to geology was the **principle of uniformitarianism**. "Uniform" means "same." Hutton's idea is that the way the Earth works today is the same way it worked in the past. In other words, rocks have always formed in the same ways. So by studying the Earth's processes today, we can also learn its history. Geologists extend this idea now to plate tectonics: we assume that tectonic plates have always been moved by the same forces.

In previous pages, we looked at how some sedimentary rocks are formed and how volcanic rocks are formed. Looking at layers of sedimentary rock, Hutton saw that igneous rock sometimes cut across it. This can happen when magma is forced up through the rock above and cools inside the Earth's crust. Hutton also recognized a third kind of rock. Where hot magma has pushed up, its heat and pressure changes the rock around it. We call these altered rocks **metamorphic rock**. "Metamorphic" means "changed shape."

Hutton's third big idea was called the rock cycle. He described how the three different kinds of rock form, break down, re-form, and change. You can learn more about the rock cycle on page 39.

↓ *A waterfall in Iceland cuts through horizontal sedimentary layers. The water carries sediment to distant places.*

↑*Ocean **waves** erode rock layers and transport sediment.*

Change Is Eternal

Sir Charles Lyell was a strong supporter of Hutton's principle of uniformitarianism. In 1830, Lyell rejected the popular idea that Earth changes because of sudden, catastrophic events like a global flood. Instead, he argued, the processes that change the Earth's surface work at a constant rate over a very long time. His ideas strongly influenced Charles Darwin, who developed a groundbreaking scientific theory regarding evolution.

"The present is the key to the past."

—Charles Lyell

"Earth has no vestige of a beginning, no prospect of an end."

—Charles Hutton

from the Crust to the Core

Making Waves

We know a lot about the Earth from what we see at or near its surface. But we cannot see what goes on deep inside the Earth. So, we only began to understand Earth's interior at the beginning of the twentieth century.

A device called a seismograph measures and records **energy** waves caused by earthquakes. In the 1880s, English geologist John Milne invented a seismograph that let researchers see different kinds of these waves. Milne got the Royal Society in the United Kingdom to place seismographs around the world. When an earthquake occurred, these machines would record how the land shook. The story they told was amazing.

Earthquake waves do not all travel the same way. Some do not pass through liquids, others do not pass through solids. From this information, geologists learned that Earth has different solid and liquid layers (see page 27).

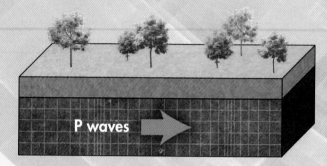

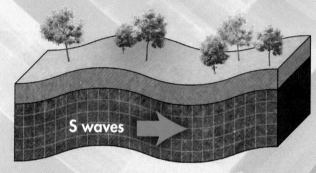

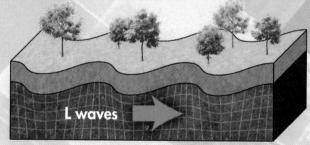

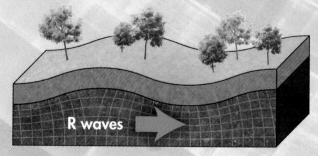

↑ *There are four types of seismic (earthquake) waves.*

Body Waves

Body waves travel through the inside of the Earth, so they tell us the most about its interior. There are two kinds of body waves.

Primary waves (P waves)

P waves are the fastest-moving earthquake waves. They travel at up to four miles (seven km) per second. P waves are also called compression waves. Stretch out a long spring. Push and pull it, then watch the wave travel backward and forward along it. That is similar to the motion of a P wave. P waves travel through the Earth. They can move through solids, liquids, and gases.

Secondary Waves (S waves)

S waves also travel through the Earth. They move at up to three miles (five km) per second. They have a side-to-side motion, like a rope being shaken back and forth. These waves move through solid rock, but cannot pass through liquids or gases.

Surface Waves

Surface waves are so named because they travel along the surface of the Earth. They are the most destructive earthquake waves.

Love Waves (L waves)

L waves have a side-to-side motion as they travel along Earth's surface. L waves move at about two miles (three km) per second.

Rayleigh Waves (R waves)

R waves are very destructive. They travel along the Earth's surface with a rippling motion, similar to waves on the ocean. R waves travel at about two miles (three km) per second, although they are a little slower than L waves.

Quick fact

A seismometer senses earthquake shock waves. A seismograph has a seismometer in it, but also an amplifier and a display that records the earthquake. The drawing a seismograph makes is called a seismogram.

A Look Inside the Earth

The Earth has four main layers. From center to surface, they are: the inner core, outer core, mantle, and then crust.

Earth's center is about 4,187 miles (6,738 km) below the surface. The inner core extends 795 miles (1,278 km) from the center. Because earthquake waves pass through the inner core, we infer that it is solid, and probably mostly made of iron. It has a temperature greater than 9,000°F (5,000°C).

From about 3,100 miles (5,000 km) to 1,800 miles (2,900 km) below the surface is the outer core. Like the inner core, it is thought to be mostly dense iron. Because secondary waves do not travel through the outer core, we know that it is liquid. Its temperature is about 7,200°F (4,000°C).

The mantle is the thickest layer and makes up about 84 percent of Earth's volume. Rock in the mantle is less dense than that in the core. It is mostly magnesium, iron, and silicon. Because of high pressure, the lower mantle is solid. Some rock in the upper mantle is molten.

Minerals harden into rock in the crust and uppermost part of the mantle. The crust is the cool, hard shell that covers the Earth. Its thickness ranges from about 0 to 25 miles (40 km). Crustal rock is less dense than that of the mantle, so continental plates float. Oceanic crust lines the ocean floors. It is mostly basalt. Most of the land on Earth is continental crust, and is mostly granite-like rock. It contains less dense minerals and so floats higher on the mantle than oceanic crust.

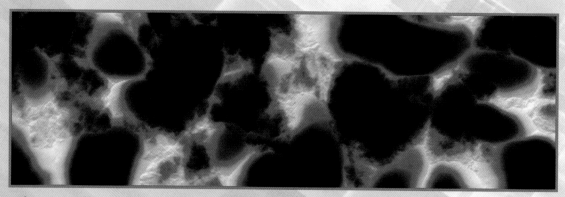

↑ The extremely high temperatures of lava cause the molten rock to glow.

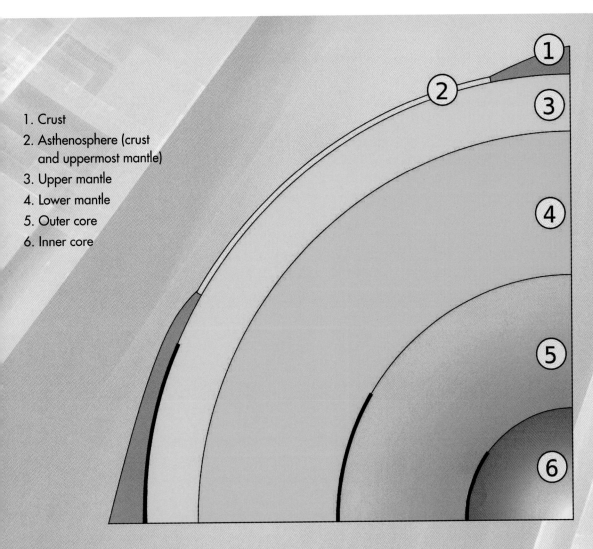

1. Crust
2. Asthenosphere (crust and uppermost mantle)
3. Upper mantle
4. Lower mantle
5. Outer core
6. Inner core

A Changing Earth

As mountains erode, rivers deposit sediments in valleys below. This explains why continents contain vast plains of sedimentary rock between vertical mountain ranges. These plains spread across North America were once vast inland seas. But why were the rock layers around some mountain ranges intensely folded?

Geologists came up with many ideas, but none answered all their questions.

Quick fact

The Mississippi River carries about 500 million tons (550 million metric tonnes) of sediment to the Gulf of Mexico every year!

Wegener's Big Idea: Continental Drift

In 1912, Alfred Wegener proposed a new idea. He had, like others, noticed that on a world map, some continents look like they could fit together like puzzle pieces. He learned that certain parts of the world have fossil records, rocks, and geological structures that match those on other continents. For example, rock layers in south Africa match those of southernmost South America. Because the fossil records and rocks are so similar, these areas of continents must have once been connected, he said.

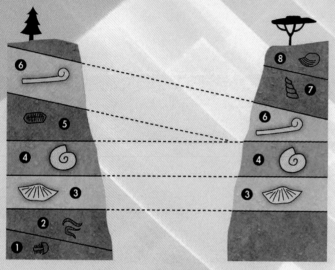

←Layers of the same rocks can be found many miles apart. By mapping them, we can figure out how they extend underground, were weathered away, or split apart because of continental drift.

Wegener combined this information in his theory of continental drift. His theory stated that the continents were once all one supercontinent, called Pangea. Over time, they "drifted" apart. Oceans flowed into the empty space between them.

↓Continent shapes are one clue about how they fit together. The fossil record also tells us that certain areas were once connected.

AFRICA

INDIA

SOUTH AMERICA

ANTARCTICA

AUSTRALIA

Other geologists combined Wegener's continental drift theory with their own evidence from rock and fossil records. This led to a more complete map of the Earth's history.

Current theory holds that Pangea began breaking up 225 million years ago. It split into two large continents. In the north was Laurasia, which became North America and Asia. The south was Gondwana, which became South America, Africa, India, Australia, and Antarctica.

Mapping the Sea Floor

In 1872, a small wooden warship called the HMS *Challenger* was sent off to study the oceans. Over four years, its crew recorded many things, including the layout of the ocean floor. Until then, humans had only observed Earth's surface above water.

Using many miles of rope, the *Challenger* crew tested ocean depths. They found underwater hills, plains, volcanoes, and deep trenches. They discovered a great undersea mountain range snaking up the middle of the Atlantic Ocean.

Despite convincing evidence, continental drift was not quickly accepted. It still left major questions unanswered.

→ *The HMS* Challenger *was painted by William Frederick Mitchell.*

Wegener's Critics

One of the biggest problems was that continental drift did not explain how the continents moved. The ocean floor is made up of solid basalt. What could possibly propel solid rock through solid rock?

Paleontologists, who study the fossil record, also dismissed Wegener at first. Species could have crossed ancient **land bridges** that spanned the oceans. Over time, as land and sea levels changed, those land bridges would have sunk under water. That could explain differences in fossil records.

Wegener couldn't answer all the questions his critics raised. He spent the rest of his life defending and trying to prove his theory. But a few geologists took his ideas to heart and continued to investigate them. Thirty years after his death in 1930, enough new information had come to light that Wegener's idea of continental drift became the Theory of Plate Tectonics.

"It is just as if we were to refit the torn pieces of a newspaper by matching their edges and then check whether the lines of print move smoothly across. If they do, there is nothing left but to conclude that the pieces were in fact joined that way."

—Alfred Wegener

↓ Limestones formed on the bottom of a sea can be found high in mountains. Minerals and fossils in rocks help us know where they formed and how they moved.

Geysers

Aristotle once called geysers "the exhalation of the Earth." Today we know they are not caused by wind blowing beneath the crust. They are caused by heat deep inside the Earth.

Water flows beneath the Earth's surface in most places. Sometimes it flows past an area where there is hot magma. Water expands when it is heated. As it expands, it is forced upward through the crust. When it shoots out the surface as a **plume** of boiling water, it is called a geyser.

↑ *Water heated by rock underground sometimes shoots out of the crust as a geyser. Here, Castle Geyser erupts in Yellowstone National Park, Wyoming.*

On the Move

During the Second World War, technology advanced by huge leaps. After the war, geologists began using several new inventions to improve their understanding of the Earth. They were able to answer many of the questions Wegener's theory of continental drift could not.

From Wegener's early ideas, this new generation of geologists built the Theory of Plate Tectonics. This theory holds that **convection currents** and other forces in the mantle push the oceans open. As they do so, magma surfaces and hardens, creating new oceanic crust. As the oceanic crust is moved along, it collides with continental crust. The denser ocean floor usually is pushed under the lighter continental crust, and melts back into the mantle.

Two more key advances led to the modern Theory of Plate Tectonics: sonar and paleomagnetism.

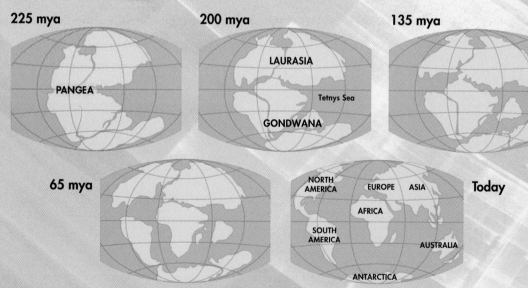

225 mya   200 mya   135 mya

LAURASIA

PANGEA

Tetnys Sea

GONDWANA

65 mya

NORTH AMERICA   EUROPE   ASIA   Today

AFRICA

SOUTH AMERICA

AUSTRALIA

ANTARCTICA

↑About 225 million years ago (mya), the supercontinent Pangea began splitting apart.

Sonar

Dr. Reginald Fessenden was a Canadian inventor working in Boston in 1913. He developed a machine that produced sound waves. When the waves hit a solid object, they bounced back. We know how fast sound waves travel. By measuring how long it took for the waves to go out and back, Fessenden could measure how far away an object was. We call this system sonar (sound navigation and ranging).

Geologists began using sonar to map the sea floor. American researchers used it on important mapping expeditions. In 1957, the world saw the first map of the ocean floor that allowed people to see what it looked like. A long ridge of huge mountains in the middle of the ocean was visible. Parallel to it were deep trenches and younger mountains. People realized that geological features matched areas where earthquakes occurred.

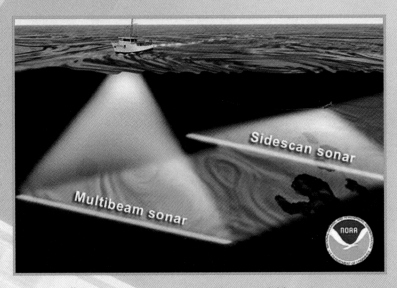

Sidescan sonar

Multibeam sonar

← Ships can use sonar to explore the seafloor.

"I had a blank canvas to fill with extraordinary possibilities, a fascinating jigsaw puzzle to piece together. It was a once-in-a-lifetime—once-in-the-history-of-the-world— opportunity for anyone, but especially for a woman in the 1940s."

—Marie Tharpe, cartographer who created the first map of the seafloor

Paleomagnetism

Earth has two magnetic poles: the north pole and the south pole. Some rocks contain minerals that line up so they point north–south. Every so often, the poles reverse. In other words, if the poles reversed right now, a compass would always point south instead of north. When Earth's poles switch, it happens fairly suddenly.

↓ *Every so often, Earth's magnetic poles reverse. We can track those reversals in seafloor rocks.*

A. Period of normal magnetism

B. Period of reverse magnetism

C. Period of normal magnetism

When magma reaches the surface and cools, the minerals in it crystallize. Until the magma is solid, magnetic minerals in it can rotate. They line up north–south. When the magma cools completely, the magnetic minerals are locked into place. In some rocks, this leaves a permanent magnetic record of where the poles were.

Geologists studied changes in magnetic records of rocks across the seafloor. These records were compared to other magnetic records from around the world. They found that the youngest rocks were near the mid-ocean ridge. The oldest were closest to the continents.

Quick fact

Earth's magnetic field reverses about once every 700,000 years on average. Rock records show it happening more than 400 times over the last 330 million years.

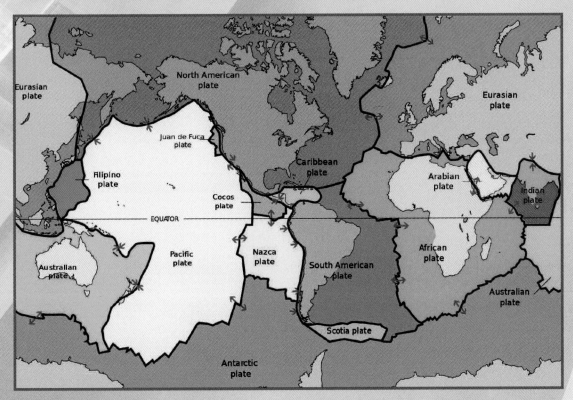

↑ Earth's crust is made up of seven major and several smaller plates. Most land occurs on six of the main plates.

Growing Oceans

By the 1960s, geologists knew that continental drift was real. The newly discovered seafloor features and earthquake data suggested that there were active boundaries between oceanic and continental plates. The paleomagnetic information confirmed that the seafloor was spreading. As more and more information about the seafloor became available, people were able to create a more detailed map of Earth's crust.

The map on this page shows the different continental and oceanic plates. The oceanic Pacific plate is mostly under the Pacific Ocean. There are six main continental plates. They include the North and South American plates, the African plate, and the Antarctic Plate. Most of Europe and Asia are on the Eurasian plate. India, Australia, and most of Oceania share what's been called the Indian-Australian plate. Current data show that the Indian-Australian plate seems to be breaking up. So, it is now often mapped as two plates.

Where Plates Meet

Tectonic plates are constantly moving. They move apart, crash together, and slide against one another. For each of those events, there is a different type of boundary. There are divergent, convergent, and transform boundaries.

Divergent Boundaries

"Divergent" means to move in different directions. Divergent boundaries occur where plates are driven apart. Partially molten material from the mantle pushes up through the surface, creating new rock. As it does so, existing rock is forced aside. Divergent boundaries occur where seafloor spreading occurs. The mid-Atlantic ridge is one example of a divergent boundary.

Most of the major divergent boundaries are under the ocean. But continents can split apart, too. Where continents split we find rift valleys. There are mildly active ones in east Africa and along the Rhine River valley in Germany. As rift valleys open, water flows into the new lowlands. The Red Sea and the Gulf of California are flooded rift valleys.

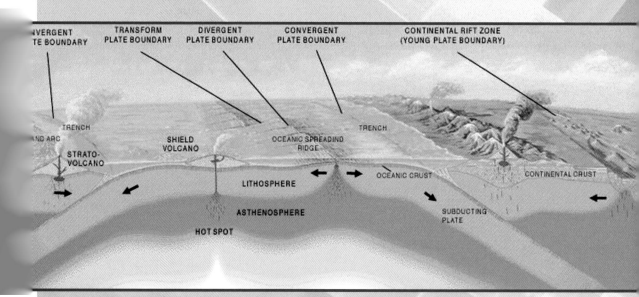

↑Divergent boundaries occur where plates move apart. Convergent boundaries occur where plates move toward each other. Hot spots can occur in the middle of a plate.

Convergent Boundaries

"Convergent" means to come closer together. While plates move outward from divergent boundaries, their other edges crash against other plates. Where two plates collide we call it a convergent boundary. Such boundaries usually involve an oceanic plate and a continental plate. The denser oceanic plate is usually forced under the continental plate. Most earthquakes and the most violent volcanoes occur along convergent boundaries.

(For more on earthquakes and volcanoes, see Chapter Five.) Continental plates collide, too. India is on the fastest-moving plate. Where the Indian-Australian plate meets the huge Eurasian plate, the Himalaya Mountains are formed. The Himalayas include some of the highest mountain peaks in the world, including Mount Everest and K2. (See Chapter Six to read about how mountains are made.)

↓Mountain ranges, such as this range in India, can occur where plates converge.

Transform Boundaries

In some places, two plates slide past one another instead of crashing together. These areas are called transform boundaries. The San Andreas Fault in California is a famous transform boundary between the Pacific Oceanic plate and the North American plate.

↑The Rhine River Valley is a minor rift valley.

Pushing the Plates

We know that plates move apart and can open up in the middle and break apart. We also know that they crash into and grind against one another. But one of the biggest questions Wegener's critics asked remains: What makes these huge sections of the Earth's surface *move*?

This question has been a source of great debate. We know from seismic studies that there is a plastic, or semi-liquid, layer of the mantle under the crust. We call it the **asthenosphere**. Because it is composed of partly melted rock, it can flow.

The deep mantle is very hot, and heat rises. Near the surface, the rock begins to cool and eventually begins to sink back down into the Earth. It does this in circular motions called convection currents. If you want to see convection currents, fill a glass with very hot water and drop in a little food coloring. You will see the color rise and sink as water of different temperatures circulates in the glass.

As rock circulates across the top of the mantle, it drags the crust along. A plate is pushed in the direction of the mantle current below it. Divergent boundaries are where two currents move in opposite directions. These currents also drag pieces of crust down at convergent boundaries.

Jet-like plumes that rise from the edge of the outer core may also play a role in continental drift. We do know that features called kimberlites are remnants of such plumes.

↑A form of mining called strip mining is sometimes used to access kimberlites. Strip mines are vast, open pits in the Earth's surface.

Quick fact

Kimberlites are a kind of rock formed deep in the mantle, where there is intense heat and pressure. Most diamonds are found in kimberlites.

The Rock Cycle

Rocks form, break apart, and change in a process known as the rock cycle. New igneous rock forms when magma reaches the crust. At the surface, it begins to erode and become sedimentary rock. Heat and pressure can change either type into metamorphic rock. And all three types can be eroded into sediment, or pushed back under the earth and melted.

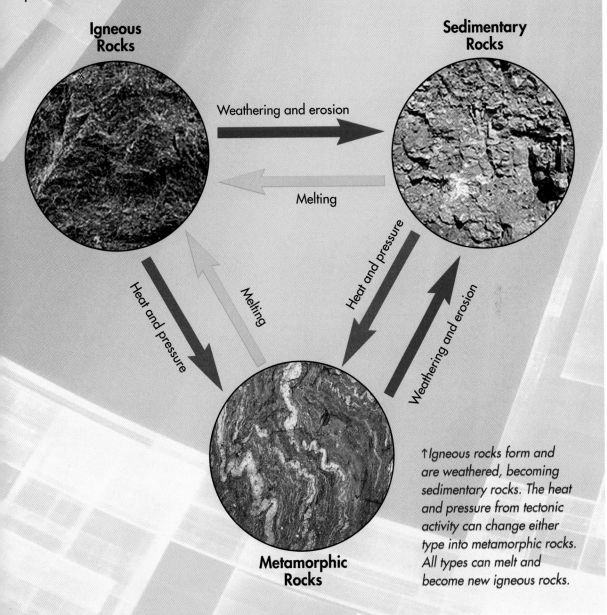

Igneous Rocks

Sedimentary Rocks

Weathering and erosion

Melting

Heat and pressure

Melting

Heat and pressure

Weathering and erosion

Metamorphic Rocks

↑Igneous rocks form and are weathered, becoming sedimentary rocks. The heat and pressure from tectonic activity can change either type into metamorphic rocks. All types can melt and become new igneous rocks.

Making Mountains

When plates collide, they do so with enough force to thrust up huge mountains. Most mountains are formed in one of two ways: through subduction or accretion.

Subduction

Subduction is the downward movement of the edge of a plate into the mantle below another plate.

Subduction occurs where ocean floor and continent meet. Continental crust moves up over the oceanic crust. The oceanic crust is pushed down into the hot mantle. Because oceanic crust carries water with it, some of the rock melts (water lowers rock's melting point). The melted material, or magma, rises up through the continental crust, melting some continental material along the way.

Some of the magma cools inside the crust. This is where metamorphic rocks form. Some magma bursts through the surface, creating volcanic mountains. Subduction can also happen when two pieces of oceanic crust meet. As one plate is forced down under the other, an arc of volcanic islands results. (See Chapter Six for more information about volcanoes.) Sometimes two pieces of continental crust collide. An ocean between two pieces of continental crust will slowly close by subduction.

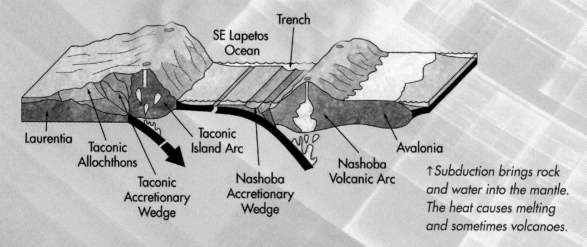

Laurentia
Taconic Allochthons
Taconic Accretionary Wedge
Taconic Island Arc
SE Lapetos Ocean
Trench
Nashoba Accretionary Wedge
Nashoba Volcanic Arc
Avalonia

↑ Subduction brings rock and water into the mantle. The heat causes melting and sometimes volcanoes.

Accretion

As continental crust rides over an oceanic plate, it is deformed and pushed upward. Some sedimentary material from the oceanic crust will also be "scraped off" onto the continent. This material gets pushed up onto a continent in a process called accretion.

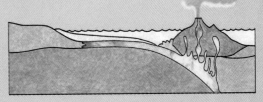

↑ Plate movement pushes a volcanic island toward a continent.

When two pieces of continental crust collide, they both resist being forced down. This is because both pieces are relatively light and float on the mantle. So, they crash together. Sections of crust get broken off one plate or the other. Movement in the mantle pulls some chunks under the other continent. Some chunks get smashed, thrust up, and accreted (attached) to the other continent. The chunks of continent that are thrust up are fractured into slabs as much as 12 miles (20 km) thick.

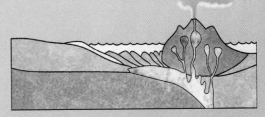

↑ The island pushes seafloor sediment and rock along in front of it.

↓ These layers of sediment and the volcanic island are eventually pushed up onto the continent.

By studying accretions, geologists figured out that there has been more than one single supercontinent, and that oceans open and close. Eastern North America has acquired pieces of crust that originally were part of Europe and Africa.

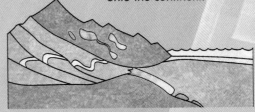

"With such wisdom has nature ordered things in the economy of this world, that the destruction of one continent is not brought about without the renovation of the earth in the production of another."
—James Hutton, *Theory of the Earth*

The World's Great Mountains

Mountains provide some of the planet's most breathtaking scenery. There are major mountain ranges on every continent.

Mount McKinley, Alaska, U.S.A.

Mount McKinley, also called Denali, is the highest mountain in North America. Its peak has been measured at 20,320 feet (6,194 m) above sea level. It formed 56 million years ago as magma that cooled inside the crust and was thrust upward when the Pacific and North American plates collided.

Aconcagua, Argentina

The highest mountain in the Americas is Aconcagua. Its peak is 22,841 feet (6,962 m) above sea level. It is part of the impressive Andes mountain range that runs along the west coast of South America. It was pushed up by tectonic activity, although there are volcanic rocks on the mountain.

Quick fact

The peak of Mt. Everest is the highest point on Earth's surface, measured from sea level. But measured from base to peak, Hawaii's Mauna Kea is the tallest mountain on Earth.

Matterhorn, Switzerland/Italy

At 14,692 feet (4,478 m), the Matterhorn is not the highest peak in the Alps. But its steep, four-sided peak is one of the most famous in Europe. The Alps are a mountain range stretching across France, Switzerland, Italy, Austria, and Germany. The Alps formed when Europe and Africa collided 65 million years ago.

Mount Everest, Nepal/Tibet

Famous as the world's highest mountain, Mount Everest's peak is 29,029 feet (8,848 m) above sea level. Straddling the border of Nepal and Tibet, Everest is part of the Himalayan Mountains. The Indian-Australian plate moves faster than most plates, at six inches (15 cm) a year. It crashed into the huge Eurasian plate 50 million years ago, forming the Himalayan Mountains.

Mount Kilimanjaro, Tanzania

The slopes of Mount Kilimanjaro are famous for coffee as well as climbing. It is a massive volcanic mountain, with a peak 19,336 feet (5,895 m) above sea level. It stands alone, the only mountain on a vast plain in east Africa. The last volcanic activity on the mountain took place 200 years ago.

Mountains and Their Rocks

All rocks are made up of minerals. Igneous rocks are mostly made up of minerals containing silicon. Granite, basalt, and obsidian are all silicate igneous rock. Granite has large crystals, forming from magma that slowly cools in the crust. Basalt forms when magma cools quickly, as with lava spewing from a volcano. It has smaller crystals.

Most sedimentary rock comes from mountains being weathered and eroded. The pieces, or clasts, settle as sand, silt, or gravel, in lakes and oceans. Sandstones and siltstones form from sediments.

Other sedimentary minerals are dissolved during weathering and later precipitate out, when water evaporates. Calcite is one such mineral. Limestone is a sedimentary rock made from calcite.

Metamorphic rock is any kind of rock that has been changed by high temperatures and pressures. At plate boundaries, heat and pressure bend or fold rock over large areas. Igneous granite can become metamorphic gneiss with visible bands of quartz and mica.

Sometimes metamorphism occurs in a small area, like the area around an igneous intrusion. Rocks that come into contact with the hot magma are partially melted. This contact metamorphism turns sandstone into quartzite or limestone into marble.

←A close-up of granite shows that its crystals are relatively large compared to basalt, another igneous rock.

Quick fact

Obsidian is an igneous rock. It forms when molten rock cools so quickly that it cannot crystallize. When broken, it has a circular fracture, much like thick glass.

↓Fossil shells are sometimes preserved in sedimentary rock.

↑A close-up of marble shows how minerals have been partially melted and recrystallized.

Life on a Mountaintop

Animals and plants living on mountaintops have to adapt to the cold and the rough terrain.

Harsh weather and thin soils mean there are no trees. Shrubs, grasses, and herbs are most common in the pockets of soil between hard rock. In some places, only lichens and moss-like plants cling to the rocks.

↑High in the mountains, lichen such as red-tipped Cladonia cristatella grow among plants only inches high, and ice, wood, and rocks.

Nimble mountain goats may graze the alpine meadows. Falcons enjoy the safety of mountain ledges and hunt the valleys below. Creatures living on the windswept peaks, such as the hoary marmot, need thick fur to protect them. It's a harsh climate, but a truly beautiful **ecosystem**.

Explosive Earth

Plates move with tremendous force, enough to raise up mountains. The very forces that build continents can also be unleashed explosively and destructively. Plate tectonics is behind volcanoes, earthquakes, and tsunamis.

Volcanoes

As discussed in an earlier chapter, convection currents in the mantle move tectonic plates. When one plate is pushed under another, some of its rock melts and rises. This can cause a volcano. Volcanoes also occur where two plates are pulling apart or over "hot spots" in a plate.

How a volcanic mountain is shaped depends on how it erupts. Some produce thick lava that oozes out across the surface. Others have thinner lava and more gas, and explode into the sky. After many eruptions, the lava, rock, and ash that are spewed out build up in layers, creating a mountain. There are three main kinds of volcanic mountains.

The Ring of Fire

Most earthquakes and volcanoes occur where oceanic and continental plates crash into one another. The Pacific Ocean is surrounded by such plate boundaries. There are so many earthquakes and volcanoes around the Pacific that its perimeter is known as The Ring of Fire.

↑Fifteen shield volcanoes, such as this one in Hawai'i Volcanoes National Park, make up the eight main Hawaiian islands.

Shield Volcanoes

Shield volcanoes are wide, fairly flat mountain forms, shaped like a shield lying on the Earth. Runny lava, usually rich in basalt, flows out and cools in thin layers. Mauna Loa, on Hawaii, is a shield volcano.

Cinder Cone Volcanoes

Some volcanoes shoot tons of rock and ash out of narrow openings. Large pieces form steeper slopes at the top. Small rocks and ash form gentler slopes at the bottom. When most people imagine a volcano, this is the shape they think of. The cones are usually small. Sunset Crater in Arizona is a cinder cone volcano. It formed in a series of eruptions between A.D. 1040 and 1100.

Composite Volcanoes

When a volcano forms from both flowing lava and the sort of rock material from a cinder cone, we call it a composite volcano. Its sides will have alternating layers of rock or ash and lava. The result can be very large, cone-shaped volcanoes. Mt. St. Helens in Washington State and Mt. Fuji in Japan are composite volcanoes.

Quick fact

Lava and magma are not the same thing. Magma is partially molten rock material inside Earth. It is only called lava when it comes out onto the surface.

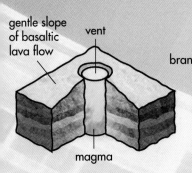

gentle slope of basaltic lava flow — vent — magma

Shield Volcano

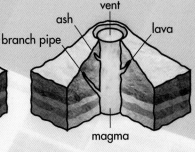

ash — vent — branch pipe — lava — magma

Composite Volcano

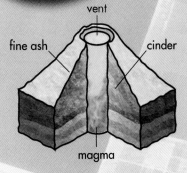

vent — fine ash — cinder — magma

Cinder Cone Volcano

Earthquakes

When Earth's plates come into contact with one another, they do not just slide by easily. Rocks are jagged. The plates grind past and press against each other. Rocks get bent until they reach a breaking point. The pressure is released violently, sending waves of energy around and through the Earth (see Chapter Three).

Most earthquakes happen at plate boundaries. Where plates pull apart, earthquakes occur near the Earth's surface. Many happen where one plate is pushing under another. There, they often happen deep underground, more than 60 miles (100 km) below the surface. Some earthquakes even happen in the middle of plates. These are near the surface and can be very destructive.

The deadliest earthquake in history happened in China, in 1556. It killed 830,000 people. But most earthquakes are not so deadly. Thousands of earthquakes happen every year. Many are so small that they cause little or no damage. Others happen deep in the ocean, where there are no buildings to collapse and injure people.

Detected only by sensitive instruments — 1.5

Felt by few persons at best, especially on upper floors — 2

Felt noticeably indoors, but not always recognized as an earthquake — 2.5

3

Felt indoors by many, outdoors by few; dishes, windows, doors disturbed

Felt by most people; some breakage of dishes, windows, and plaster — 3.5

4

Felt by all, many are frightened and run outdoors; damage small — 4.5

Everybody runs outdoors, damage to buildings varies — 5

5.5

Panel walls thrown out of frames, walls and chimneys fall; sand and autos disturbed

Buildings shifted off foundations, cracked; ground cracked; underground pipes broken — 6

6.5

Most masonry and frame structures destroyed; ground cracked, rails bent, landslides

7

Few structures remain standing; bridges destroyed, fissures in ground — 7.5

8

Damage total; waves seen on ground surface

The Richter Scale

In 1935, a California seismologist named Charles Richter developed a new scale for measuring earthquakes. A seismograph measures the shaking on the ground. The greatest amount of energy recorded by a seismograph, following an earthquake, is used to give a Richter magnitude.

Faults

The point where rocks break and earthquakes happen is called a fault. Where two pieces of crust are pulling apart, one slumps downward. This is called a normal fault.

A reverse fault is created when pieces of crust are pushed together. One will slide up the side of the other. Some reverse faults are also called thrust faults, because one piece of rock is thrust up onto the other piece.

Sometimes one piece of crust grinds past another. This creates a strike-slip fault. The San Andreas Fault in California is a famous example of this. It was created because the Pacific plate is sliding northwest past the North American plate.

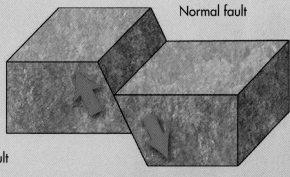

Normal fault

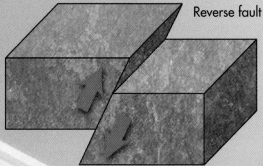

Reverse fault

Quick fact

We call the underground location of an earthquake its *focus*. The *epicenter* is the spot on Earth's surface directly above the focus.

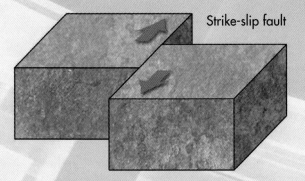

Strike-slip fault

Tsunamis

An undersea earthquake, avalanche, or volcanic eruption can cause a massive wave called a tsunami. In the past, people have sometimes called them tidal waves, but tsunamis have nothing to do with the **tides**.

Worldwide, most cities are built near water. Tsunamis can crash across an entire coastline, destroying villages. The waves can be 60 feet (20 m) tall and travel at up to 500 miles (800 km) per hour. Tsunamis are often more destructive than the earthquake or event that causes them.

On December 26, 2004, subduction caused a massive earthquake in the ocean near Indonesia. The quake measured at least 9 on the Richter scale. But the resulting tsunami is what made history. It wiped out entire communities, killing 230,000 people in fourteen countries around the Indian Ocean.

"I was with a group of my friends, playing outside, when someone said, 'What's that noise?' It sounded like thunder. ... We saw the black wave coming, high above us, and we all ran."

—13-year-old Nogadinap Priya of Sri Lanka, days after the 2004 tsunami disaster

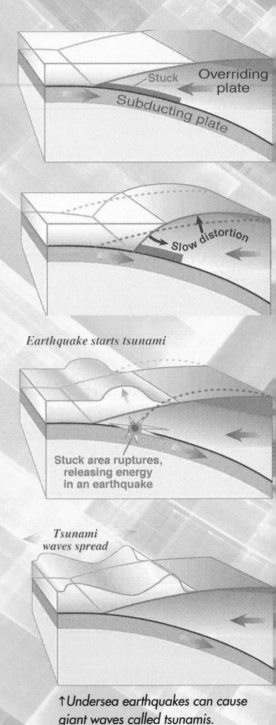

Stuck   Overriding plate

Subducting plate

Slow distortion

Earthquake starts tsunami

Stuck area ruptures, releasing energy in an earthquake

Tsunami waves spread

↑*Undersea earthquakes can cause giant waves called tsunamis.*

Three Kinds of Disaster, One Cause

Violent volcanoes, earthquakes that shake apart cities, and tsunamis that wipe away entire communities cause many of the deadliest, most destructive disasters humans experience. Ancient peoples thought their gods caused them. Some ancient philosophers thought air holding up Earth blew through the ground to cause volcanoes and earthquakes. Now we understand that all three types of potentially deadly events have one common cause: the movement of Earth's tectonic plates.

Where the seafloor spreads, magma pours out. The spreading causes normal faulting and earthquakes as the plates move apart.

Where plates meet and subduction occurs, more explosive volcanoes and earthquakes occur. Since we began to measure earthquakes that occur deep underground, we found they occur along an underground slope. As a plate is pulled under a continent, it is dragged against the crust and then the mantle. The earthquakes get deeper and deeper.

As a result, where you find volcanoes, there will also be earthquakes. If there's water nearby, tsunamis are another serious possibility.

Without these processes, however, we wouldn't have beautiful mountains. The rich soil in valleys and prairies where we grow food washed down from those mountains. Just as plate movements can kill, they provide the means for life.

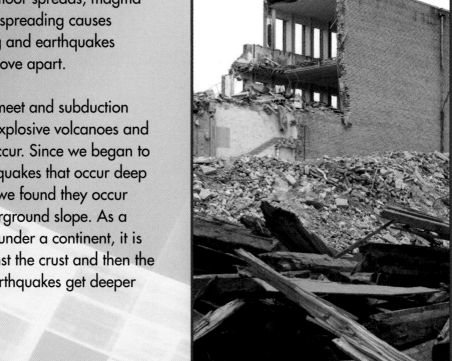

→ *Tectonic activity can greatly impact human lives.*

The Cutting Edge

Since Wegener's time, we have learned a great deal that supports the Theory of Plate Tectonics. Sonar allows us to see features on the seafloor. We looked at the orientation of crystals in seafloor rocks. This told us that rocks near mid-ocean ridges are newer than ones toward plate edges. That means plates are spreading apart. Discovering where earthquakes happen underground supports the theory of subduction.

With all this evidence, it makes the Theory of Plate Tectonics hard to argue against. Yet there is still a lot to learn.

Geologists are always looking for new ways to prove what processes move plates. They search for new evidence that will tell us more about the Earth's interior. Even new discoveries about space may lead us to learn more about our planet.

Today, some people study Earth from space. They use **satellites** orbiting 12,000 miles (20,000 km) above the Earth to measure movement of its plates. The satellites are part of the **Global Positioning System (GPS)**. It's the same system that people today use to navigate the oceans or city streets.

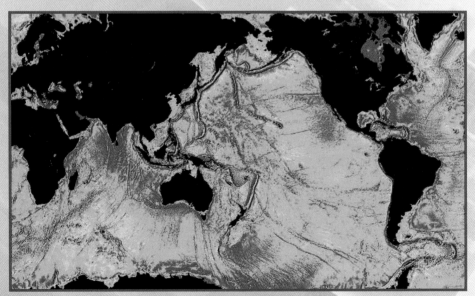

←Satellites allow us to accurately measure plate movement and also to map the ocean floor.

The United States Department of Defense has 21 satellites that send a constant stream of radio signals to Earth. On the ground, a receiver that picks up signals from four or more of the satellites can calculate where that receiver is located, including its **altitude**. That is how GPS and other space-based systems have confirmed which way and how fast plates are moving.

Satellites can also help map the seafloor. The surface of the ocean is not completely level. It bulges out over ridges and mountain chains, and drops down over deep valleys. You cannot see these differences with your eye. However, satellite-based devices can measure them.

↑ *Mars can be viewed in great detail through the Hubble Space Telescope.*

Plate Tectonics on Other Planets?

Some planets have landforms similar to ones on Earth. However, Venus does not have water, which is important in tectonic processes. Mars is thought to be too small and cold. Both planets have volcanoes, but they're extinct. It appears that Earth is the only planet in our solar system with tectonic activity.

Plate Tectonics and the Environment

The air is made up of many elements, just as rocks are. Air contains oxygen, which we need to breathe, as well as nitrogen, carbon dioxide, and sulfur. In the atmosphere, too much of one element can be a problem. Since the **industrial revolution**, more people have been using more resources. As a result, we have created more pollution.

From time to time, people have caused serious problems by releasing too much of one chemical into the atmosphere. Sulfur can become sulfuric acid and come down as acid rain. In the late twentieth century, many countries created laws to reduce sulfur emissions because acid rain was causing damage to lakes and eating away at buildings.

Today, we worry about carbon dioxide. It is one of the **greenhouse gases**. In a greenhouse, the walls let sunlight in but trap heat. In the atmosphere, greenhouse gases trap the Sun's heat. Increase the amount of these gases and the surface of Earth gets hotter. Humans produce carbon dioxide when they burn coal for energy or gasoline in their cars.

Quick fact

Plates move at different speeds and change speeds. The weight of a subducting plate section may pull the plate along. As that piece gets smaller, the plate probably slows down.

↑Mountain building, volcanoes, and erosion all play a part in nature's carbon cycle.

Nature produces carbon dioxide, too, and absorbs it. The weathering process takes up carbon dioxide from the atmosphere. Chemical reactions lock carbon into material that is eroded away. This material settles on the ocean floor and eventually becomes sedimentary rock. When the rock is drawn deep underground by subduction, it melts and carbon dioxide (along with other gases) is released and comes out through volcanoes. In this way, plate tectonics is part of the carbon cycle.

There are other natural systems that transfer carbon, too. Trees absorb it as they grow and release it when they decay or burn, for example. Burning large areas of forest means less carbon is absorbed and more is released. Sometimes the natural cycle can cause worldwide climate warming, as can happen after a large volcanic eruption. But the climate changes being observed today cannot be explained by natural phenomena. Human activities appear to have an impact on the climate as well.

A New Continent

In September 2005, the ground in Ethiopia opened up. A crack 37 miles (60 km) long began to widen. In three weeks, the sides moved apart 26 feet (8 m). Magma squeezed up into the new rift.

Rifting occurs where plates pull apart. A continental plate appears to be breaking apart under Ethiopia. It could mean the beginning of a new ocean. Or northeast Eritrea and Ethiopia may no longer be part of Africa in the future, but part of a new continent. A rift valley runs through eastern Africa, from Mozambique to the Red Sea. But it is rare to actually see a continent being pulled apart. Most rifting takes place under the ocean.

This new opening lets geologists study the process much more directly.

↓Erta Ale in Ethiopia is a shield volcano located within the Great Rift Valley. Shown below is one of Erta Ale's lava lakes.

Earth in the Future

Scientists at the University of Texas took what is known about plate tectonics and created a map of the world in the future. On the map, the Mediterranean Sea is gone. Don't worry, though; this will take 50 million years.

Because they know how fast seafloors are spreading and where plates are likely to collide and change direction, scientists can plot where continents will end up. The Atlantic Ocean will keep spreading. Africa will push further into Europe, building the Alps into a mighty mountain chain like the Himalayas are today. Australia will catch onto the tip of Asia and begin to rotate.

Beyond 50 million years, it's harder to predict what will happen. We know that continents sometimes change direction. It has happened in the past, so it is likely to happen again. But exactly how and when are questions yet to be answered. That said, the same researchers think Earth will be one supercontinent again in 250 million years.

↓ 50 million years from now, Earth's continents and oceans will be arranged and shaped differently.

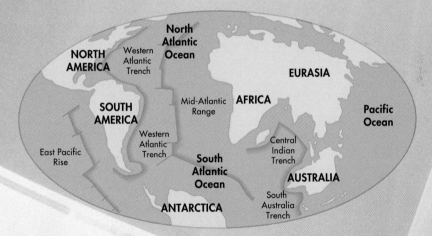

"We do not know if an ocean will eventually be formed here, but the prospects are good. It just may take a million years before the port can be built."

—Dr. Tim Wright, researcher, Leeds University, talking about the Great Rift Valley in eastern Africa

Timeline

500 B.C. Anaxagoras describes spinning universe with Earth at center

350 B.C. Aristotle discovers Earth is round and fossils that suggest erosion

240 B.C. Eratosthenes uses math to calculate size of Earth

20 A.D. Strabo writes *Geography*

79 A.D. Mt. Vesuvius erupts

1480s–1500s Leonardo da Vinci studies fossils, rejects idea of early Earth being covered in water; he does not publish this idea

1543 Nicolaus Copernicus writes that Sun is center of universe

1556 Deadliest earthquake in history kills 830,000 people in China

1669 Nicholas Steno rejects idea of water-covered Earth, explains law of superposition and principle of original horizontality.

Early 1700s Abbé Anton Moro identifies distinct origin of volcanic rock

1774 Abraham Werner publishes first textbook on describing rocks by their minerals; uses law of superposition to separate igneous and sedimentary rocks.

1793 William Smith begins dating rocks by fossil record

1795 James Hutton publishes *Theory of the Earth*, introducing principle of uniformitarianism

1830 Charles Lyell's *Principles of Geology* rejects global flood, supports constant change

1872 HMS *Challenger* begins four-year mission to map ocean floor

1880s John Milne invents seismograph

1880s Giuseppe Mercalli begins developing scale to describe earthquake intensity based on observations of destruction

1912 Wegener introduces the ideas of continental drift and the original supercontinent, Pangea

1913 Dr. Reginald Fessenden invents sonar machine

1935 Charles Richter develops Richter scale for measuring earthquakes using seismography

1956 P.M.S. Blackett invents a new, more sensitive seismometer

1957 First map of ocean floor produced using sonar

1957 Russia puts first satellite, Sputnik I, into space

1958 U.S. begins developing satellite navigation system, GPS

1963 Seismometer detects changes in seafloor magnetism, proving that seafloor spreading occurs

1970s Satellites first used to track continental drift

2004 Deadly tsunami kills 230,000 people along coasts of 14 Asian countries

2005 A 37-mile crack opens in Ethiopia; geologists can see continental rifting in action

2010 Eyjafjallajökull erupts in Iceland; ash cloud stops air travel for weeks

Glossary

altitude Distance above sea level

asthenosphere The uppermost layer of the mantle, where it is hot enough that rock can melt

continent A very large area of land. The seven continents are Africa, Antarctica, Asia, Australia, Europe, North America, and South America.

convection current A pattern of movement caused by the transfer of heat within a liquid or gas. Because heat rises and cold sinks, these currents have a circular motion.

crystal The three-dimensional solid shape a mineral forms when it cools. Most rocks are made up of crystals formed by several minerals.

deposition The laying down of earth materials. When wind or water slows, any dust, sand, or gravel it picked up falls and settles, or is deposited.

dynamic Relating to continuous change, activity, or movement

eclipse The blocking of light from one space object when another object passes between it and the observer. A solar eclipse occurs when the moon passes between the Earth and the Sun, casting a shadow over part of the Earth.

ecosystem An area that includes all the plants, animals, and non-living natural things, such as sand, rocks, and soil

element Each of more than one hundred chemical substances that cannot be broken down into a simpler substance without changing how it acts; each element has a certain number of protons, neutrons, and electrons. Atoms of elements combine to form molecules. For example, two hydrogen atoms can combine with one oxygen to form water. Elements are described and classified on the Periodic Table of Elements.

energy The ability to work or move. Most energy comes from the Sun's rays. Energy can be stored in plants, fossil fuels, or animal cells.

erosion The breaking off and transportation of particles of rock or soil, usually by water, wind, or ice

fossil Remains of an ancient plant or animal that have been buried and preserved in or as rock

geology The study of Earth, mainly through rocks, and how it has shaped and changed

Global Positioning System (GPS) A network of satellites used to locate points on Earth

greenhouse gases A group of gases in the atmosphere that trap heat close to Earth's surface; examples include carbon dioxide, methane, water vapor, and gases used in aerosols called chlorofluorocarbons

igneous rock Rock formed when magma or lava cools

industrial revolution A period in the nineteenth century when inventions such as the steam engine and machines, along with the widespread use of coal as an energy source, allowed goods to be produced in factories in great amounts

land bridge A ridge of land connecting two continents

landform A physical feature of the Earth's crust, such as a mountain or valley

mass The amount of matter an object contains. Weight is the measurement of mass within the Earth's gravitational field.

metamorphic rock Rock that has been changed by heat and pressure

mineral A naturally occurring solid with a particular chemical and crystalline composition. For example, quartz, feldspar, and mica are minerals that make up the rock granite.

nuclear reaction Atoms splitting apart and releasing energy, which smashes into more atoms, causing them to split

oblong When a circle, square, or sphere is slightly stretched in one direction

orbit The path of a planet around a star, or of a moon or other satellite around a planet

petrified Something that has turned into stone

plume An upward flow of molten rock through the mantle

principle of uniformitarianism The idea that the processes changing the Earth today are the same as those that did so in the past. Originally, the principle also stated that these processes worked at a consistent speed, but we know now that is not always so.

revolve To move in a circular orbit around a center point or another object. For example, planets revolve around a star.

rotate To move in a circle around a center line (axis) or point. For example, a planet rotates on its axis.

satellite An object in orbit around a planet, whether natural (a moon) or human-made (a communications satellite)

sediment Rock and organic material that has been deposited away from its source

sedimentary rock Rock formed when weathered or eroded material has been deposited, buried, and then cemented or squeezed into a solid layer.

solar system A group of objects, dust, and ice in orbit around a sun. Our solar system includes planets, dwarf planets, asteroids, comets, and meteoroids.

tides Tilting of seas caused by the moon's gravitational pull. Because seas tilt, on a given shoreline, the water level will rise and fall twice a day.

universe All existing things. The universe contains many galaxies, each of which contains many solar systems.

uplift The upward movement of a large section of the Earth's crust, typically at least 300–600 miles (500–1,000 km) across

wave A continuous, rippling disturbance of particles in a substance as energy (motion, heat, or sound) moves through it

weathering The breakdown of rocks on Earth's surface

For More Information

Books

Gleason, Carrie. **Geothermal Energy: Using Earth's Furnace**. Crabtree Publishing, 2008.

Gurney, Beth. **Sand and Soil**. Crabtree Publishing, 2005.

Morganelli, Adrianna. **Minerals**. Crabtree Publishing, 2004.

Smithsonian Institution. **Earthquakes and Volcanoes**. Harper Collins, 2008.

Websites

This Dynamic Earth: The Story of Plate Tectonics
http://pubs.usgs.gov/gip/dynamic/dynamic.html
Read more about plate tectonics in this online edition of a United States Geological Survey (USGS) book, **This Dynamic Earth: The Story of Plate Tectonics** by W. Jacquelyne Kious and Robert I. Tilling. Washington, DC: U.S. Government Printing Office, 1996.

Understanding Volcanoes: Lava Flow
http://dsc.discovery.com/videos/understanding-volcanoes-lava-flow.html
Learn more about volcanic activity and Earth's history in a series of videos that explore volcanic events that have affected people around the world.

Ocean Explorer **http://oceanexplorer.noaa.gov/welcome.html**
This website of the National Oceanic and Atmospheric Administration (NOAA) connects students and teachers to current research being done by ocean scientists.

Understanding Earthquakes **http://projects.crustal.ucsb.edu/understanding/**
This website, hosted by the Institute for Crustal Studies at the University of California at Santa Barbara, provides links to quizzes, information, videos, history, and literature about earthquakes.

Fossilization **www.tyrrellmuseum.com/research/fossilization.htm**
Read about the different kinds of fossils and how they are formed. The Royal Tyrell Museum in Alberta, Canada, is home to the fossils of many dinosaurs and other extinct critters.

Continents in Collision: Pangea Ultima
http://science.nasa.gov/science-news/science-at-nasa/2000/ast06oct_1/
Read more about plate tectonics and how Earth's surface may look millions of years in the future.

Earth Observatory: The Carbon Cycle
http://earthobservatory.nasa.gov/Features/CarbonCycle/
Find in-depth information about how the element carbon moves through and affects the Earth system.

Index